how to speak ■■
emoji

Fred Benenson

Andrews McMeel
Publishing®

a division of Andrews McMeel Universal

Andrews McMeel Publishing
a division of Andrews McMeel Universal
1130 Walnut Street, Kansas City, Missouri 64106

www.andrewsmcmeel.com

16 17 18 19 20 TEN 10 9 8 7 6 5 4 3 2 1

ISBN: 978-1-4494-7802-5

Library of Congress Control Number: 2016931058

First published in Great Britain by Ebury Press,
an imprint of Ebury Publishing
A Penguin Random House Group Company

ATTENTION: SCHOOLS AND BUSINESSES
Andrews McMeel books are available at quantity discounts with bulk purchase for educational, business, or sales promotional use. For information, please e-mail the Andrews McMeel Publishing Special Sales Department: specialsales@amuniversal.com.

contents

introduction

You are about to embark on a journey to the forefront of human communication in the twenty-first century: emoji. Consider yourself an early adopter.

Emoji originated in Japan and, as such, they're tightly coupled with the country's traditions, food, and culture. But since being adopted into Unicode (an effort to standardize how software interprets and stores letters and characters) and integrated into smartphones, they're now everywhere, used around the world by young and old alike. Sometimes they communicate our feelings when text won't do, other times we use them to tell stories, and sometimes we just like to test our friends and family with emoji puzzles.

I first discovered emoji in late 2008, when using them required downloading a special Japanese iPhone app to unlock the emoji-only keyboard. I became obsessed with writing full sentences in emoji and sending them to everyone I knew.

I wondered whether I could write a whole story in emoji, but then thought it might be more interesting to translate a book everyone already knew. Pushing the idea to its limit, I chose Herman Melville's *Moby Dick*, and hired a small army of Web workers to crowdsource the project. In late 2010, I self-published

Emoji Dick, and the book has since taken on a life of its own—in 2013 it was acquired by the US Library of Congress as their first emoji-only book, and it has been called everything from a tragedy to a masterpiece.

I'm now frequently asked whether I consider emoji a language. That's a hard question to answer and the best I usually come up with is "Not yet." Which is where this book comes in. That people are even raising this question testifies to the fact that emoji are playing an increasing part of our day-to-day communication and, arguably, functioning something like a language.

This book contains some common (and uncommon!) phrases translated into emoji. And just like any other spoken-language phrasebook or dictionary, these pages do not (and cannot!) supply the whole possible range of emoji usage you might encounter, but they're a tool you can use.

The Austrian philosopher Ludwig Wittgenstein famously argued that natural language is comprised of games, where we learn the meaning of words through their usage and context in life, just like the way we learn the rules of a game by playing it. I think that this is an apt way to think of emoji: Right now, they may *feel* like a game, but we're actually using them to convey complex meaning and nuance.

The rules of this game are just beginning to emerge and I hope you'll join me in what is bound to be an exciting development in the future of communication.

basic language tips

There are a handful of ways to think about emoji translation. Here's a couple of the techniques I used to make this book:

- Literal translation: Sometimes you find the exact emoji you need—for example, 👽 for the movie *Alien*—and at other times you need a handful.

- Rebus: When an emoji is used to replace a word or part of a word. For example, 🔍 + 📅 = Friday.

- Visual pun: Using emoji to imply a different meaning than originally intended. For example, 🥒 for . . . well, you can guess.

- Telling the story: Sometimes you can take it a bit further and play out your intended meaning. So for "break the ice," I've had the emojis act it out: 🏃 🔨 🧊 .

To make your own emoji translation, get creative! Don't worry about verbs or abstract concepts, focus on clever pairings, use literalness when you can (e.g. "shooting pain" uses 🔫 to convey the word *shooting*), and don't be afraid to use the emoji with words in them (e.g. 🔜). Finally, have fun and don't take it too seriously; chances are people will understand the general gist of what you're trying to say and you'll get points for being creative regardless.

emoji dictionary

One of the originals and still one of the most frequently used emoji, this one works when you're simply feeling happy.

 Currently the most popular emoji on Twitter, this one is typically used to convey "LOL" or "I'm laughing so hard, I'm crying."

 There's some confusion about why this face is both smiling and sweating, but this is the perfect emoji to use when expressing relief.

 For when you're smitten, or just very grateful.

 For when things are .

 This emoji's name is "confounded face," but it's best used to illustrate complete emotional disintegration.

 A not-so-subtle way of conveying affection. Useful for arranging second or third dates.

Techinically named "pouting face," this one is surely better at conveying anger.

 Widely known as "sob emoji" this is perhaps more useful for insincere commiseration.

 The "cold sweat emoji" can be used to convey absolute desperation and/or fear.

 If you find yourself extremely shocked, this is a perfect emoji to use—it's loosely based on Edvard Munch's famous painting *The Scream*.

 Ever get blackout drunk? This emoji is for the next morning.

 It's unclear why we need cat variations of emoji faces, but probably useful if you're a cat lady.

 When you want to say "no" as emphatically as possible. It can be paired with 🚫 for extra effect.

This emoji is supposed to mean "bowing deeply," but is commonly used to express gratitude or surprise.

 Begging, praying, giving thanks, high-fiving, worshipping—one of the most versatile emoji.

 Unicode 8.0 included a new set of same-sex couples, as well as varied skin tones for commonly used emojis.

 The raised fist can be useful when communicating political messages via emoji.

 Going to the gym, feeling powerful, a vague threat—the muscled arm can be used in a variety of contexts.

 Need to point something out?

Victory or peace?

It's unfortunate that these eyes only look left, but pair this with another emoji when you need to keep an eye on something.

 For when you're feeling petulant—or you can pair this emoji with basically anything else to convey your desire to lick it.

Night and day. If you're going to reference the moon or the sun, why not choose the ones with a face?

 Typically used to symbolize friendship, this emoji derives from Japan's Bunny Woman, which is based on the Playboy Bunny.

 For your special day. Unless you have ginger hair, in which case you are not represented.

It is almost impossible not to offend when using this emoji.

 Useful if you'd like to call your lover "baby," or if you just think he or she is behaving immaturely.

My angel! Another good one to send to your special someone.

 "What's the deal?"

 A beefeater emoji! Although obviously recognizable to Brits, sometimes this emoji is used to symbolize a "sketchy guy" in the US.

 Ideal for organizing a fun night out.

 Useful when you're late, or keen to see someone.

 Ooh, fancy!

 One of twenty-five clock faces available in emoji. This is also used to advertise Apple's new watch.

 The name of this emoji is "snowman without snow"—so what is it made from? Handy for denoting that you're freezing.

When you've forgotten a Valentine's present, there's a large array of flora on offer.

When a kissy emoji just won't do . . . 😉

Combine this with a question mark and you've got dinner planned! Also, it's the closest emoji to cheese, and as such, is used frequently.

Can be brought out on Friday night, often followed by a string of all the alcohol emojis on offer.

Hungover? Bad acne? Use this guy.

There is no crab emoji, but in a pinch, the dragon one can be used to point out how touchy your friend is being.

Has a naughty alternative meaning.

Why are there two camel emojis when there isn't a crab one?

 This can be used to imply hard drugs or the need for medical attention.

 For when you've got a bright idea or as an if there's a power failure.

 Literally used, this emoji can suggest a night of billiards, but it can also be deployed if your friend is being cryptic.

 Another highly versatile emoji, the flame can be used to connote sexiness, anger, or heat.

 This emoji is named "splashing sweat," but can really be used for any bodily fluid.

Love hotels are popular short-stay hotels in Japan that can be rented for the hour, so you can use this emoji to suggest a saucy rendezvous.

Does this emoji refer to wind? Or farts? Or fog? As it turns out, it works for all three.

 The money-with-wings emoji can be used in a variety of contexts to connote everything from high prices to taxes to party time.

 A twin of the original *Space Invaders* character, is is typically used to refer to video games.

 Use the fax machine, minidisc, or pager to gently rib your friends that their tastes— in technology or otherwise—are completely outdated.

Could this emoji be used to represent emoji itself?

A subtly saucy combination.

This emoji's name is "hocho," which is the name of an all-purpose knife common in Japan, but it can be useful if you want your message to appear more threatening, particularly when combined with the gun and/or bomb.

 This emoji is your best shot for "stone." It actually represents a Moyai statue in Tokyo, despite being commonly called the "Easter Island emoji."

 Some emojis have words in them, which you might consider cheating, but you'll find them very useful at times.

 There's no emoji for fingers crossed or a middle finger, so why not suggest your grudging approval with this emoji?

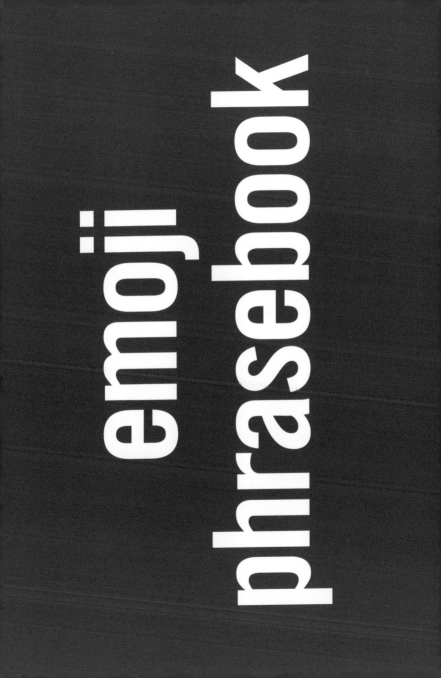

emoji phrasebook

Basic
Conversation

Good morning!

Yo, baby.

What's up?

Good-bye!

Excuse me.

Cool story, bro.

It's Friday!

Hey, boy. / Hey, girl.

Shoot the breeze.

Ooh, epic fart!

It's written in black and white.

 🐼

Let's break the ice.

 🔨 🏊

Please?

🙏 😁

How are you?

😄 ↔️ 😣 **?**

Great!

😎 😊 👍 🎿

Not so good, I need a drink.

I'm a happy camper.

Right as rain.

Hold the phone.

Mic drop!

Slug it out.

He would say that, wouldn't he?

Let's take a rain check.

Holy crap!

Don't have a cow!

What's the scoop?

 ?

I have to shove off.

I don't have the foggiest idea.

Idioms

A fool and his money are soon parted.

Lightning never strikes twice.

Cleanliness is next to godliness.

In one ear and out the other.

"Abandon hope, all ye who enter here."

how to speak emoji phrasebook

It's darkest just before dawn.

You're barking up the wrong tree.

Hedge your bets.

That's a piece of cake.

Out of the frying pan and into the fire.

how to speak emoji phrasebook

Hook, line, and sinker.

That's what she said.

All that glitters is not gold.

Aim for the stars!

The best things come in small packages.

A leopard can't change his spots.

Like a lamb to the slaughter.

Don't throw the baby out with the bath water.

Let sleeping dogs lie.

Cat got your tongue?

how to speak emoji phrasebook

Don't get your panties in a twist.

Beauty is in the eye of the beholder.

Every dog has its day.

They went eyeball-to-eyeball with each other.

An elephant never forgets.

I've got to go see a man about a dog.

Above and beyond.

Come down to earth.

A little bird told me . . .

Go forth, divide, and conquer!

Absence makes the heart grow fonder.

A chain is no stronger than its weakest link.

Don't cut corners.

Actions speak louder than words.

Hit the nail on the head.

If the mountain will not come to Muhammad, Muhammad must go to the mountain.

As exciting as watching paint dry.

Don't count your chickens before they hatch.

Funny as a barrel of monkeys.

Beggars can't be choosers.

Building castles in the sky.

Don't cry over spilled milk.

Ace in the hole.

A sticky situation.

When pigs fly!

A pig in a poke.

Don't be cheeky.

One-upmanship.

Food
and Drink

A watched pot never boils.

This egg might be past its use-by date. . . .

I feel like chicken tonight.

Ew! Bad chicken!

Finger lickin' good!

I could kill for a glass of wine.

I'm carrying a little water weight right now.

I'm hungry!

I'm on a diet.

I'm no longer on a diet.

I'll have two beers, please.

Can you make it as spicy as possible?

What do you fancy?

Eat, drink, and be merry, for tomorrow we die.

I am on a liquid diet.

Is this really beef?

I'll have the surf and turf, please.

You can't have your cake and eat it, too.

There appears to be an insect in my soup.

I'll never eat baby octopus again.

Never eat sushi from a gas station.

Your friends are terrible cooks.

That was the worst meal I've ever had.

That was the most amazing meal I've ever had.

Can I have the bill, please?

Relationships

Can you cook dinner? I owe you one!

You're a catch!

Can you play music loudly so I can go to the bathroom?

I'll never look at another woman again.

Hi, honey!

how to speak emoji **phrasebook**

You're a bombshell!

Sexy beast.

Silver fox.

Can you choose something on Netflix already?

You are smoking hot, sweetheart!

It takes two to tango.

Enjoy your bachelorette party!

He's a real ladies' man.

Fancy meeting you here.

I'm head over heels.

Do you love me?

I would like you to meet my parents.

When can I see you again?

It's been a real emotional rollercoaster.

Can we be friends with benefits?

She charmed the pants off me.

Whose lipstick is on your collar?

I have many sexually transmitted diseases.

Sorry, I am engaged.

Next time I'm in town, I'll drop you a line.

how to speak emoji phrasebook

I love you to the moon and back.

A dozen roses.

I had to kiss lots of frogs to find my prince.

Let's get freaky!

My girlfriend is a bit younger than me.

Pickup
Lines

Is this your lucky night?

How big is it?

You've got a great pair.

I bet you're an animal in the sack.

Are you a racehorse? Because you've been running around my head all night.

What a meat market . . .

I'm having a whale of a time!

I'm writing a phone book. Can I have your number?

Wanna hump?

Might not be the best idea . . .

Do you believe in love at first sight, or should I walk by again?

Do you live in a cornfield? Because I'm stalking you.

Did you have lucky charms for breakfast? Because you look magically delicious!

Is your dad a thief? Because he stole the stars and put them in your eyes.

Does your left eye hurt? Because you've been looking right all day.

Is your dad a drug dealer? Because you're so dope!

I must be a snowflake, because I've fallen for you.

Was your dad a baker? Because you've got a nice set of buns.

Was your dad a baker? Because you've got a nice set of buns.

All I want for Christmas is you.

I love animals.

I was feeling off today, but you turned me on.

I'll cook you dinner if you cook me breakfast.

I don't have a library card, but do you mind if I check you out?

Insults

Grow some balls!

Suck it up!

A prize fool.

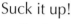

Two wrongs don't make a right; take your parents as an example.

You bore me to tears.

You're a pill.

Go f*ck yourself!

Your family tree is a cactus because everyone on it is a prick.

You're a pain in the ass.

I find your opinions outdated.

Kiss my ass!

Cry me a river.

Ambulance chaser.

Oh, go row a boat.

That's a game two can play.

It looks like your face caught on fire and someone tried to put it out with a fork.

He's a bull in a china shop.

Crocodile tears.

🐊 😩

Don't call me, I'll call you.

📱 ✋ 📞 👉

Do I have to paint you a picture?

😔 🎨 📷

Excuse my French!

It's a case of the blind leading the blind.

I may love to shop, but I'm not buying your bullshit.

Gasbag.

Nightlife

What fool wears sunglasses at night?

Not sure these drugs are working. . . .

#YOLO

Last night, a DJ saved my life.

The night is young!

Let's get drunk on sake and sing karaoke!

The drinks here are too expensive.

What time is last call?

Cirque Du Soleil

Let's go back home, this party sucks.

DJ, play my song!

But I'm on the guest list.

Put me in a taxi, I'm drunk.

This crowd is a little young for me.

Do you know where I could find some medicinal marijuana?

Put on your dancing shoes.

If you slip the bouncer twenty bucks, we'll get in.

Drink all day, party all night.

I don't go to clubs.

The line for the women's bathroom is ridiculous.

Famous
Quotes

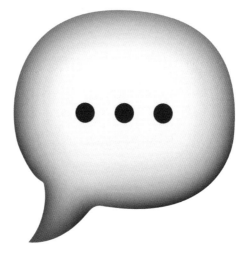

"If opportunity doesn't knock, build a door."
MILTON BERLE

"A camel is a horse designed by committee."
PROVERB

"Don't cry because it's over, smile because it happened." DR. SEUSS

"All's fair in love and war." FRANK SMEDLEY

"God save the Queen." BRITISH NATIONAL ANTHEM and

SEX PISTOLS

"Dance like nobody's watching, love like you'll never be hurt, sing like there's nobody listening, and live like it's heaven on earth." WILLIAM W. PURKEY

"That which does not kill us makes us stronger."
FRIEDRICH NIETZSCHE

"Comedy is tragedy plus time." STEVE ALLEN

"Let them eat cake." MARIE ANTOINETTE

"Nobody puts Baby in a corner." DIRTY DANCING

68

"The early bird might get the worm, but the second mouse gets the cheese." UNKNOWN

"Better to remain silent and be a fool, than to speak and remove all doubt." MAURICE SWITZER

"Time and tide wait for no man." PROVERB

"How do you like them apples?" *GOOD WILL HUNTING*

"Beauty awakens the soul to act." DANTE

how to speak emoji **phrasebook**

Lyrics

"I see trees of green, red roses too."

LOUIS ARMSTRONG

"Pretty fly for a white guy." THE OFFSPRING

"Come on baby, light my fire." THE DOORS

"Love is a battlefield." PAT BENATAR

"We found love in a hopeless place." RIHANNA

"When the moon hits your eye like a big pizza pie." DEAN MARTIN

"A hard day's night." THE BEATLES

"Everyday I'm shufflin'." LMFAO

"Lonely as I am, together we cry."
RED HOT CHILI PEPPERS

"It's raining men." THE WEATHER GIRLS

"Don't look back in anger." OASIS

"Last Friday night." KATY PERRY

"Baby got back." SIR MIX-A-LOT

"Party in the USA." MILEY CYRUS

"Drunk in love." BEYONCÉ

"The eye of the tiger." SURVIVOR

👉 👀 🐅

"We are never ever ever getting back together."
TAYLOR SWIFT

Film and
TV Titles

Star Wars

Alien

Requiem for a Dream

Planet Earth

The Office

The Godfather

Boyhood

3rd Rock from the Sun

Girls

Trainspotting

Fight Club

Orange Is the New Black

Beauty and the Beast

The Shining

Mad Men

Game of Thrones

Friends

Breaking Bad

Help and Directions

Where's the best place for dancing?

Where is the nearest bathroom?

Which way to the Sistine Chapel?

Where's the red-light district?

I'm lost. Where is Bear Grylls?

I'm looking for the nearest race track.

Can you show me where the campus is?

How far away is the nearest oasis?

Do they speak French in Canada?

You can go on foot.

Crosswalk.

I'm looking for the post office.

Turn left at the traffic lights, love.

Is there a good Chinese restaurant?

Does a troll live under that bridge?

I don't know. You'll have to ask someone else.

Where can I rent a car with more horsepower?

It's a dead end.

Err . . . it's not *too* far from here. . . .

In the Workplace

Bathroom emergency!

Blue-sky thinking.

Did you attend the sexual harassment sensitivity training workshop yet?

Make the intern do it.

Don't leave a paper trail.

Sorry I'm late, my train was held up!

The big cat upstairs likes to blow his own horn.

Someone finally recognized all my hard work.

I really need to hit my bonus this year.

We need to square the circle.

He's such a joker!

TGIF!

I'm out of the office. I will respond to any e-mails on my return.

I'll be working from home today.

It's a dog-eat-dog world.

A long, boozy lunch.

That deal was fishy. We need to cover our tracks.

If I don't stay late, the boss is going to fire me.

He's a snake. Keep your distance.

You're going to smash this pitch!

Stop hogging the company credit card!

That's why they call it happy hour.

Nah, I don't do meetings.

This venture is going to be a gamble.

The coffee here is crap.

😨 ☕ ➡️ 😵 💩

Did you watch last night's episode of *Doctor Who?*

👀 📺 ❓ ⏳ 🔄 ⏳ ☎️ 👽 👮

My boss just added me on Facebook.

👴 👔 👥 👍 ❓ 😟

The fax machine seems to be possessed.

📄 📠 🔥 😈 🔥

That's his problem.

🙈 🙉 👉 💥 👉 👤

91

how to speak emoji phrasebook

Let's take this conversation offline.

Thinking outside the box.

Did you get the memo about the TPS reports?

Technology

I got an upgrade!

Technophobe.

Have you turned it off and back on again?

Lets just play video games all day.

I love surfing the Web.

Your computer has many viruses, please don't send me any e-mail attachments.

Nice Apple Watch.

He's got an electric car.

My neighbor bought a satellite dish to communicate with aliens.

Inbox ZERO!

how to speak emoji phrasebook

Ah! Where's my charger?

My new subwoofer will blow your mind.

Encryption.

I've got that movie on Blu-ray.

I need my card reader.

Megabyte.

Cyberbullying.

Motherboard.

Let me just burn these files onto that disc.

Are you on LinkedIn?

What's the bandwidth?

Keywords.

I'll find you on Facebook.

I've got a match on Tinder.

Clip art.

Is it inkjet?

Caps lock.

PowerPoint.

Travel

The London Eye.

The best way to learn a language is on your back.

Dear Dad, I'm running out of money for traveling and I would appreciate your assistance.

I'm going backpacking in Southeast Asia for six months.

how to speak emoji phrasebook

My malaria pills are giving me weird dreams.

The journey of a thousand miles begins with one step.

The journey of a thousand miles begins with one step.

I don't know what to do with all this foreign currency.

I need the first ticket out of here.

Are there toilets at the top of the Statue of Liberty?

I took the sleeper train last night and feel like hell today.

Don't tell anyone about my secret surf spot.

Disaster tourism is so passé.

I've lost my passport and need to visit the embassy.

Missed the bus.

Do they have Uber here?

Hotel is booked up, let's find a campsite!

Paris is most beautiful in the rain.

Do they have Kit Kats in France?

I'm so happy to be home!

Medical/ Emergency

Where can I buy some earplugs?

Am I under arrest?

My child is missing.

There's a gang of wild cats terrorizing my neighborhood.

He was captured by headhunters.

I don't remember where I was last night.

I got my wisdom teeth out.

Does it smell like something is burning?

EARTHQUAKE!!!

I think I swallowed a bone!

how to speak emoji **phrasebook**

I think I ate the wrong piece of the blowfish.

I can pick any lock!

Uh oh, out of gas.

It's coming out both ends.

I'm not a licensed medical professional, but you should get that checked out.

Do you know if they'll have to amputate?

Is she dead?

I got mugged and I can't pay for dinner.

Fire!

My husband got apprehended at customs.

how to speak emoji **phrasebook**

My roommate was abducted by aliens.

I recorded the accident on video and will send it to my insurance company.

The way to subdue an alligator is to wrestle it and rub its belly.

I've got a shooting pain in my foot.

I've lost my birth control pills!

It's so swollen!

It hurts here.

I've lost all control of my bladder!

Do you have a painkiller?

My teeth are wobbly.

I think I have food poisoning.

I think I broke my arm.

It's contagious.

Weather

Cold hands, warm heart.

It's so hot you could fry an egg on my forehead.

It's raining cats and dogs.

I'm just singing in the rain.

Did you see that shooting star?

Tomorrow, there will be a full moon!

The calm before the storm.

There's not a cloud in the sky.

Raindrops keep falling on my head.

A storm is brewing out at sea.

I'm walking on sunshine.

It's fine! It's just drizzling. . . .

What's the weather forecast?

We're snowed under!

There's a southwesterly breeze.

It's positively tropical out there!

We'd better run for it!

It's so foggy you can hardly see your hand in front of your face.

It's a perfect day for all sun worshippers.

Mother Nature is on the warpath.

A howling wind.

The houses are getting hammered by storms.

A mackerel sky.

Red sky at night, shepherd's delight.

They're predicting record highs!

Seasonal

New Year's Eve.

St. Patrick's Day.

Day of the Dead.

Valentine's Day.

Groundhog Day.

how to speak emoji phrasebook

Mardi Gras.

Fourth of July.

Indian summer.

Hanukkah.

Christmas comes but once a year.

Halloween is the best holiday.

The dead of winter.

Earth laughs in flowers.

God rest ye merry, gentlemen.

I've got spring fever!

April showers bring May flowers.

Dog days of summer.

As a child, I wasn't allowed to celebrate Halloween.

The Twelve Days of Christmas

On the twelfth day of Christmas, my true love
gave to me . . .

A partridge in a pear tree.

Two turtle doves.

Three French hens.

Four calling birds.

how to speak emoji **phrasebook**

125

Five golden rings.

Six geese a-laying.

Seven swans a-swimming.

Eight maids a-milking.

how to speak emoji phrasebook

Nine ladies dancing.

🕺🕺🕺🕺🕺🕺🕺🕺🕺

Ten lords a-leaping.

🚧🏃👑🚧🏃👑🚧🏃👑🚧
🏃👑🚧🏃👑🚧🏃👑🚧🏃
👑🚧🏃👑🚧🏃👑🚧🏃👑

Eleven pipers piping.

Twelve drummers drumming.